i

CORPORATE STUFF

Laments of a BurnOut

By

Chris Kay

Illustrated by Madilyn Stein

Fame's Eternal Books, LLC
United States of America

CONTENTS

Dedication

In loving Memory of my Mother,
Phyllis Kay,
who always encouraged me to
believe in my dreams;
and to
Don Krasen,
who always stood by me
and encouraged me
to achieve my dreams and to write.

Acknowledgments

I would like to thank all my friends and family for their encouragement through the years. I am very grateful to Don Krasen, who always cheered me on and encouraged me in every way. I am honored and indebted to my illustrator and friend, Madilyn Stein, for doing far more than I ever could have asked. She brought life to my words and saw the humor in them. I am also very grateful to my publisher, Tammy Maté, for encouraging me to do the book from the very first moment she saw it.

Foreword

It is hard to explain, but the "corporate thing" or "corporate world" is not a group or company. It is an energy all its own. It has become an invisible force that controls all who work in a corporate environment. However, the "corporate monster" is a tyrant with no name or face that seems to drive us all. No one knows who or what "it" is. There seems to be a whole set of unspoken rules and regulations that we all understand. It is explained as "That's how it is done in the corporate world." I worked with wonderful people who were very good to me. This book expresses my own frustrations under the tyranny of the "corporate monster," which in reality is in my mind.

Introduction

It is all a big irony, perhaps a cosmic joke, that I have worked for corporate America. I took great pride in studying liberal arts and had absolutely no interest in taking business courses. Although, one year I did get it in my head that I should get with the program of life and "get a job" in the "real world."

I went out and bought a beige suit. I got a peach colored blouse that had a little hanging bow in front. I got my resume copied onto the perfect off-white—or should I say—beige paper. I remember looking around the room full of aspiring applicants one day and feeling existential despair.

Everyone had on beige suits with peach blouses. Everyone had beige resumes. For a moment, I felt beige as I sank into a colorless world of nothingness.

I didn't get hired there in corporate America or in any of the social work jobs I thought would be meaningful. One day, I saw an ad to work in a vitamin shop. I decided to apply, and thought I would find work related to my hobby since I couldn't get hired in my field—or the "real world."

As I said, I was sick of the beige suit. I put on a silk dress with a sea of Monet-like colors. I put on red snakeskin high heels. I got hired in the natural foods industry.

It's been years since that day. I thought I was spending my life on the fringes of society working in a marginal field. Instead, I worked in a world of meaning—promoting health and wellness. Some days, I even felt like Ponce de Leon's representative in the modern day world. In reality, whatever the reason or illness that draws one to the natural foods industry, it boils down to the ideology of "the fountain of youth." We sell the Holy Grail filled with pills, potions, lotions, and elixirs. We use words such as energy, health, vitality, anti-aging, longevity, etc.... This is a feel good society.

The family owned company that I worked for was purchased by a large corporation. I was swept into corporate America without even applying for it. Mind you, I was probably calling on a store wearing Teva sandals when this happened. I guess I finally did "get a job" in the "real world."

Chris Kay

XV

CORPORATE STUFF

Laments of a BurnOut

Thank You Starbucks

I am sure I couldn't do my job without Starbucks.
It is the first thing on my mind when I awake.
I stand in line with other ambitious people
waiting for my serving of the magical blend.
Wonderful coffee beans selected from around
the world are there

Just For Me.

Listening to everyone order all the fabulous elixirs
and the sound of the coffee being poured while
cappuccino steams...is like music while I wait my turn.

Thank You Starbucks.
I feel great!

4

Starbucks

I fantasize working
at Starbucks
and serving the
hot brew to all
those who rush
off to make the
corporate machine run.

I will greet them
with the warmest smile,

because I know.
I will be the highlight
of their day!

5

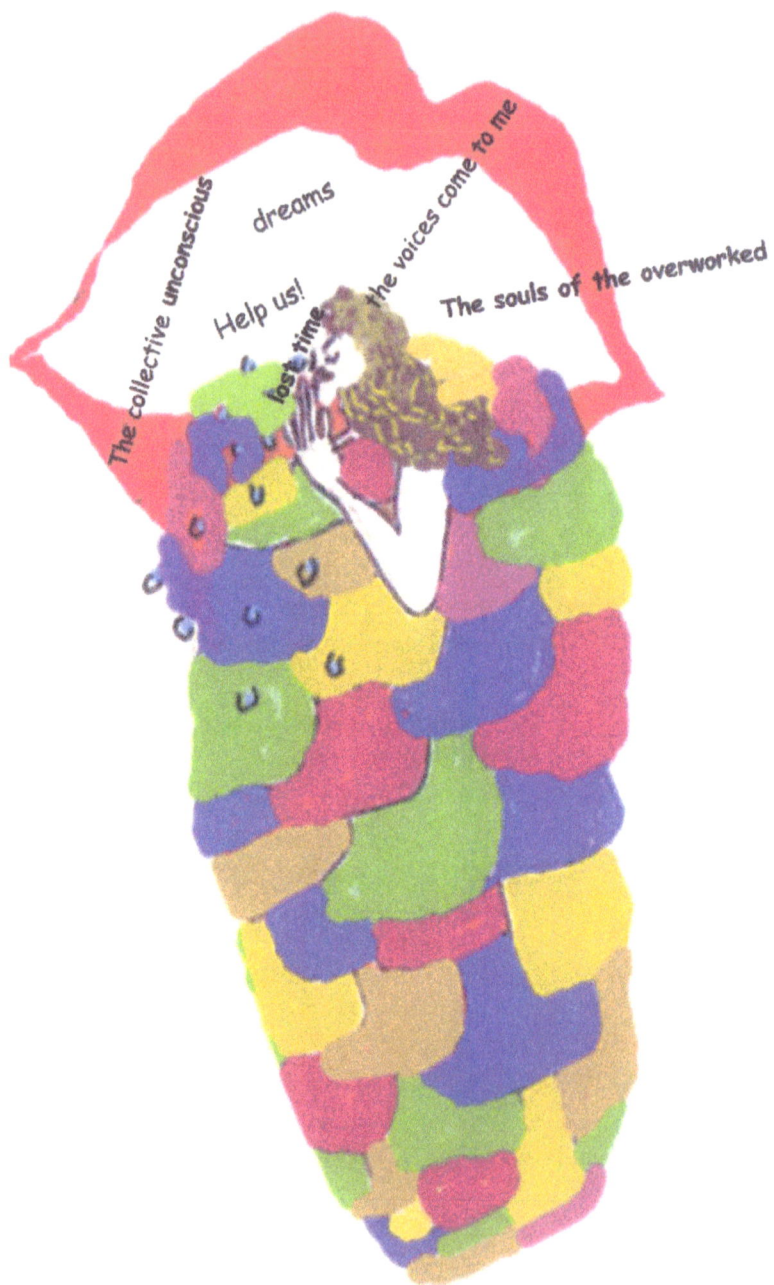

The collective unconscious

dreams

Help us!

lost time

the voices come to me

The souls of the overworked

6

The Voices

I want to dream
beautiful dreams
and write
pretty stuff.
But when I sleep
the voices come to me
and beg me
to be the voice of all tired overworked Americans.
They cry for the lost time with their families and
friends. Help Us! Help Yourself!
The collective unconscious brings the words to me.
The souls of the overworked Americans drown in
the oppression of too
much work and too
little time.
It is the hope that
the words will set us free.

Go For It

While chasing the elusive American Dream
many willingly go through the doors into the
Corporate Machine.
Suddenly it is prison...
a very big one.
We look for an escape and wonder whatever
happened to our own dreams.

8

10

The Corporate Graveyard

Behind the big fancy buildings
hiding in cubicles are the living dead
dressed up in blue suits.
Having spent a decade building a career
and having gone as far as possible up the ladder
they sit quietly—not causing waves
hoping not to be in the
next round of downsizing.
Anyone who has survived has paid.
They are dead—the living dead.
They have lost their souls,
creativity,
inspiration,
and big pieces of their humanity.
They think they will start to live when they retire and
can reclaim their lost selves.
Often it isn't long before they are buried.

Suits of Clothes

Success is like a suit of clothes.
It has a certain look. It wears an attitude.
likewise...
failure!
It has a certain look.
Can I change who I am?
like a suit of clothes?
Change a thought?
Change an attitude?
Is the thinker or the thought who I am?

Seduction

It sounds so very good that everyone envies your success:

Company Car
Salary + Commissions
Company Credit Card
Stock Options
401K

I cry at night.

You Are Hired

Look at Me.

The Corporate

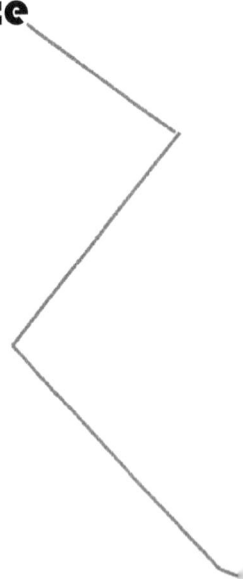

Employee!

Buy Out

I had a dream job working for a family owned business.
I loved going to work.
I was swept into Corporate America
when the family business sold.
Now the Corporate machine pounds
blood from my flesh

and makes up stuff for me to do.

I wonder if
they were aware
that I would do

All they ask Anyway?

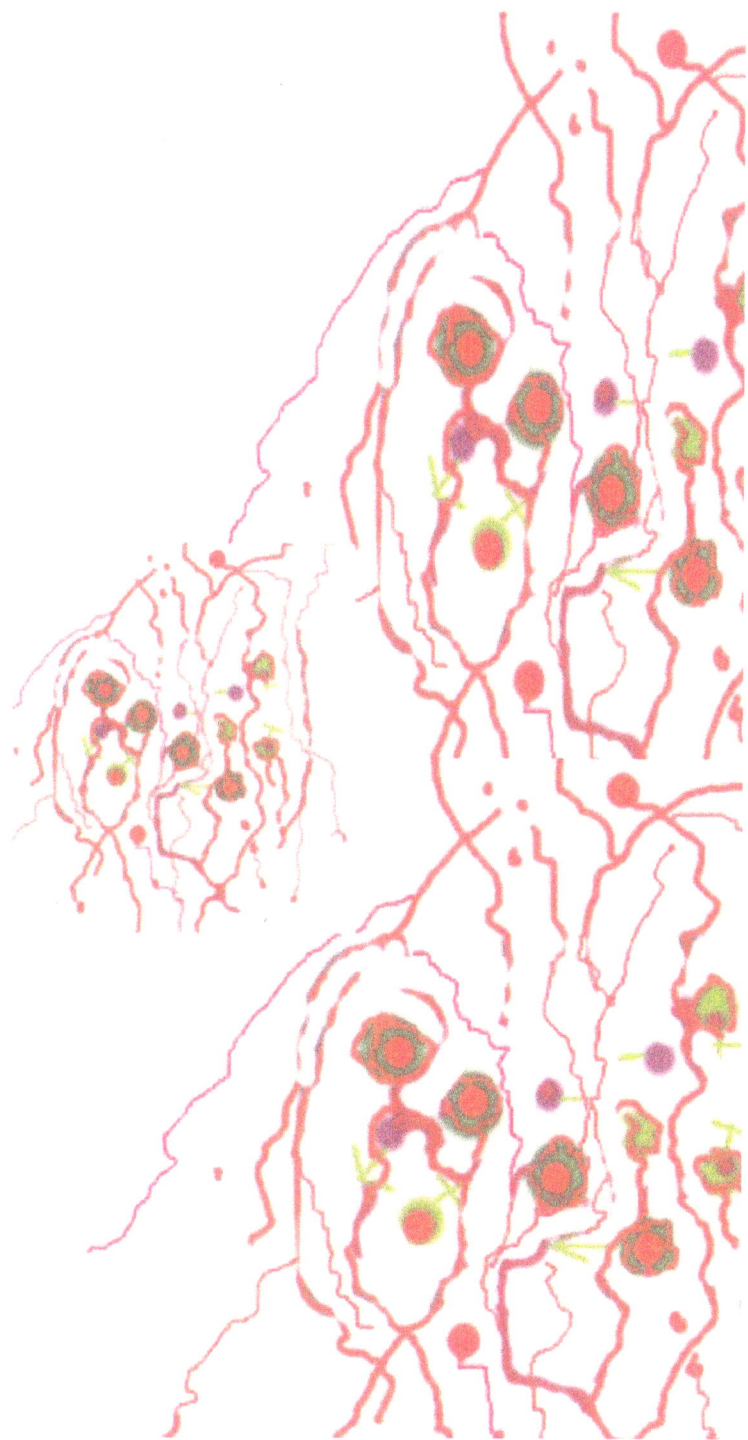

library Shelves

Thousands of us are to be put on library shelves.
We aren't books—we are career profiles.
The library shelves are now just spaces
on a hard drive.
I'm in a section or file called "aging" and "gender
bias."
Not many will find me there. They are not looking.
I want to be under "adventure" or "creativity," but in
Corporate America these qualities go to a wasteland.

Reports

While we spend so much time documenting and filling out reports, the job could have been completed many times over. Now I actually don't have time to do my job!

Reports

Reports

Reports

Reports

Report.

Reports

Reports

Reports

Lost Sales

Positions have been dissolved.

People have quit.

Sales are down.

What to do?

Show Up

There are more theories on "How To Sell"

and

"How to Motivate the Sales Force."

There are books – more books and

those consultants who are

paid big bucks to tell us how to

do "it" better.

The same old thing works every time, though:

Show Up!

Go see the customers.

Be of service.

Be nice.

Be honest.

Have integrity.

They will buy every time.

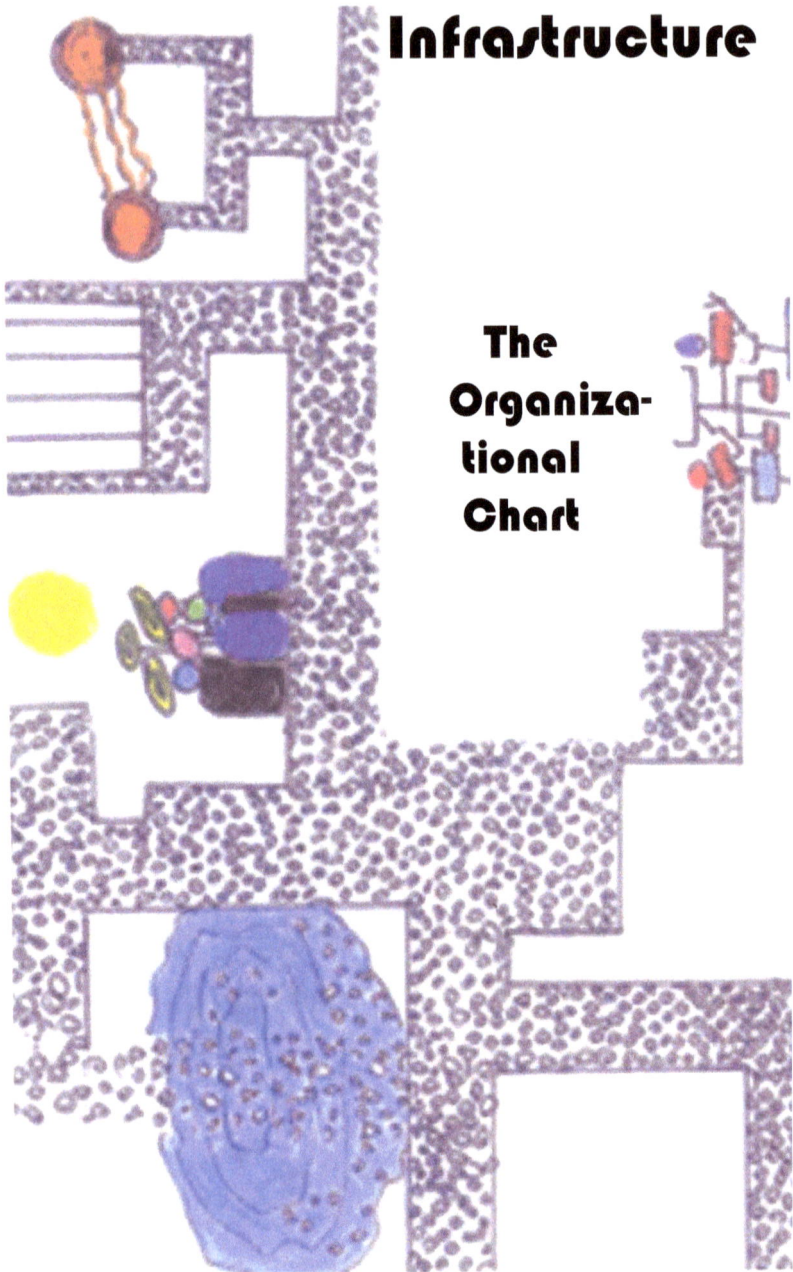

Infrastructure

The Organizational Chart

Infrastructure

There are now so many people
working that they are lost in
the maze. It takes a very long
time to weave through the
chain of command.
Once it took five
minutes with a phone
call to complete a
task.
It now takes a week
for each person to
pass things through
the
organizational
chart.

E-mail Rain

Pellets of e-mail rain daily.
Some days, it pours.
Phantoms I don't know sit in cubicles
creating e-mails.
It gives them something to do
while I work my buns off.
Before e-mail, I got my job done.

creating emails

Get rid of recipes!

get well

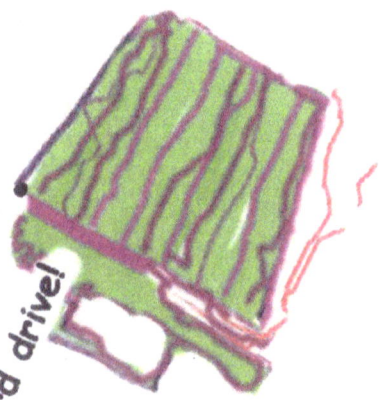

release

Etc...

Clean out your hard drive!

Etc...

Delete Photos!

release

recipes

The E-mail Police

Clean out your hard drive!

Get rid of recipes!

Delete Photos!

Etc...

let go

Aftermath

After the buyout
a co-worker said
he was on drugs,
alcohol, and
antidepressants...
and that was just to go to work!
We laughed wildly,
in stitches,
uncontrollably,
and we knew it was true.

33

Straight Jacket

I am bound in a straight jacket.

They have me bound so tight.

I can't move.

I can barely breathe.

They SQUEEZE...

the life from me.

Corporate
Stuff

Corporate stuff is getting to me.

I'm tired.

I'm overworked.

A person can't win.

I'll never be enough.

There is no end.

I'm tired of the corporate stuff.

I won't try to explain.

The corporate stuff is in my head

while I sleep and while I eat.

My body is tired. I go to bed tired.

I wake up tired, and my brain is dull.

I thought I really could fit in and did pretend.

By some measure I was good.

Though, it was a clue it didn't work

when I wished for a

valium patch and a vacation at a mental institution.

36

mental vacation

institution

Valium Patch

37

Stress Relief

I drink coffee until I shake!

My hands shake as I pour

another cup.

My heart races.

I feel great!

I feel great!

Corporate Tyrant

"In my mind" there is a
Corporate Tyrant.

He
watches
everything
I do.
Even when I'm off
he thinks I should work.

42

What Does It Mean?

**Money has danced such a seductive
dance that all of America
has such lust and
comes up wanting and
so deeply unsatisfied.**

43

Don't Quit Your Job!

I work in the sweatshop of Corporate America.
No one thinks of it as so.
It appears that auto deposit, company cars,
company credit cards, and a 401K have paid the
price for our servitude.
These benefits have bought our weekends, mornings,
and night. 9-5 is a fantasy and 24-7 is how it is.
Many of us can't sleep,
so we work in the middle of the night.
We can't eat,
so we work at lunch hour.

My therapist and friends say,
Don't Quit Your Job!

Your Job

What's Enough?

I drink coffee until I shake.
I started drinking coffee with adults when
I was four or five. It was laced with sugar
and milk. I guess you could say it was a latte.
I feel comforted when I drink coffee.
Those memories are dear.

Later in life when I was older
and getting myself upset,
Mama would say,
"Take a bath and relax.
Get yourself a cup of coffee."

So when I am stressed,
I drink coffee to calm me.
I sit and wonder, "What really is enough?"

46

Sensory Deprivation Vacation

I need a *sensory* deprivation vacation.
I am over-stimulated and on
sensory overload.
I am in need of
medication or
perhaps
intoxication.

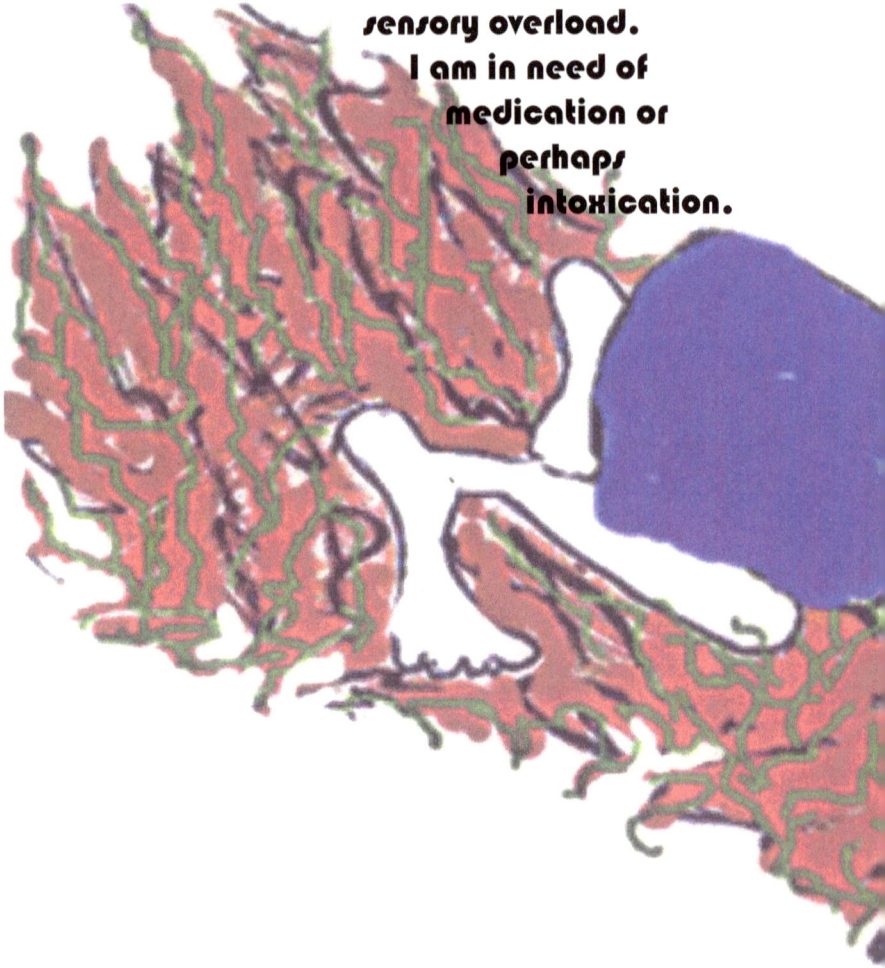

I
Need
a
Sensory
Deprivation
Vacation

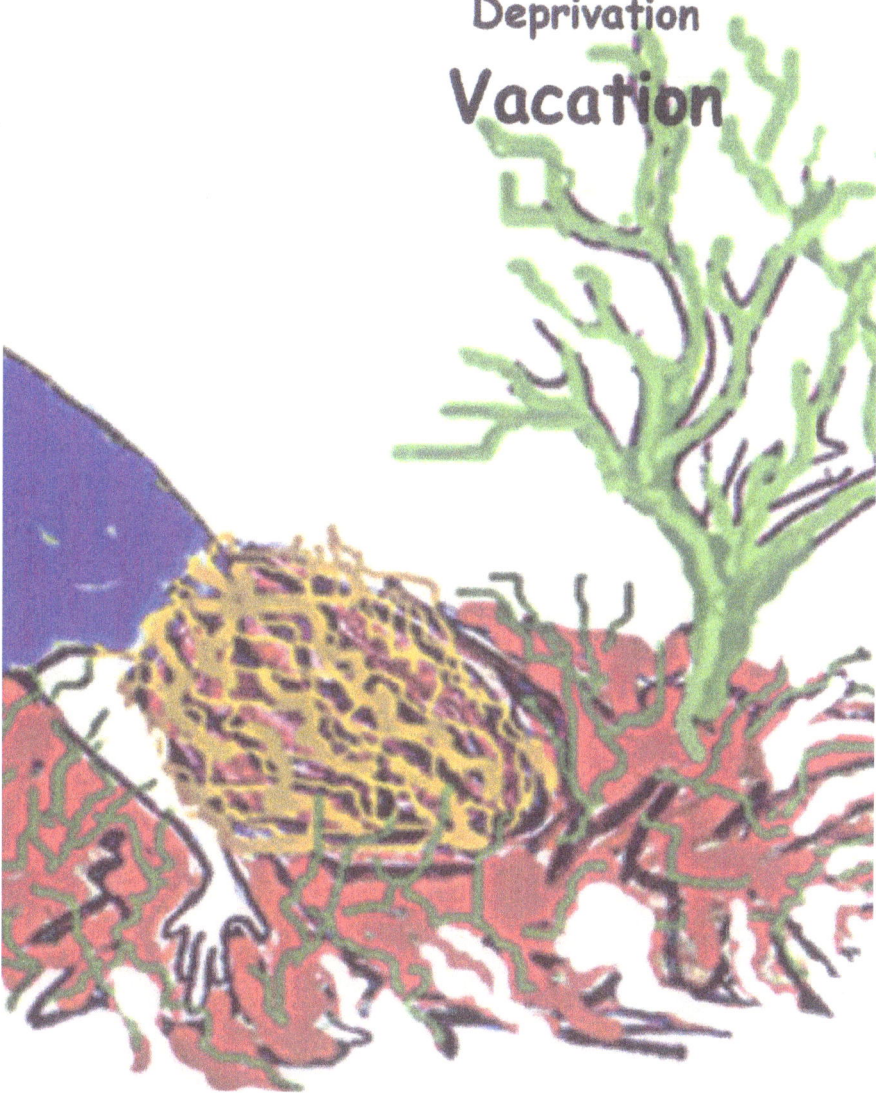

49

LayOffs

LayOffs

LayOffs

I envy those lucky ones
who have been set free
with severance pay.

I love pink –

I think I'd even like

a pink slip.

Not a silk one with lace,
but one wrapped in a nice

Layoff Package.

50

Pink Slip

51

You are fired!

This was tuff. It hurt our egos,
but we got the message
LOUD AND CLEAR.
Now everything is polished.
Positions are dissolved.
Your job simply no longer exists.
The company has restructured.
Your job just isn't there.
It has vanished in thin air.
You are given a little "package,"
so that you can leave knowing
they took "care of you."

"Thank you"

"Thank you"

"Thank you"

Voices In My Head

The voices in my head are speaking to me.
The voices in my head say, "Want to be free?"
"Tell the people they want to be free."
The voices in my head can't be me.
Who are the voices speaking to me?
Oh my! The collective unconscious is speaking to me.
Am I crazy – out of my mind?
Oh my. I think it is reality.
I'm beat – trying to sleep,
but the voices keep talking to me:

Speak the pleas of humanity.
Set the overworked American people free.
Write the words. The words will set them free.
Blow them to the wind. Tell a friend.
Stir the dust of contempt. Let the revolution begin.
We want to sit on the porch with a friend,
read a book, and chat with a neighbor again:
sing a song: say a prayer:
build community for our heirs.
We want time on our hands to hang around.
We want time on our hands – time to spend.
We want to contemplate existence again.

Oh my!

54

write

time

contempt

friend

revolution

sing

crazy

beat

voices

overworked

unconscious

pleas

free

chat

humanity

read

The collective unconscious is speaking to me.

Willie Loman

I was talking with Willie Loman today.
He says I don't have much time.
He is the guardian angel for salesmen.
He is the forlorn prophet who only speaks to us.

When I was younger, "Death of a Salesman" was
a play by Arthur Miller. Now Willie Loman thinks
he is my best friend – a self appointed mentor.

Not so long ago, he was just an occasional
ghost – barely visible, who sometimes scared me.
Now he is the phantom who sits beside me as I
ride up and down the highways from town to town.
He is an invisible presence that speaks so loudly,

"Beware! Beware!"

"Death of a Salesman"

Resignation Letter

I am the human flesh that feeds the Corporate Monster.
The ravenous creature eats pieces of me daily.
My mind, body, and spirit are the energy
that fuel the insatiable appetite.
I am breakfast, lunch, and dinner.
I am snacks in between.
I die daily.
He's never satisfied.
He never sleeps.
I die daily
as he eats more & more until
I am gone...
I taste stale.
It doesn't matter now.
As there is always
New
Flesh
To
Feed
The
Beast!

Good - Bye

It is with joy and glee that I say good - bye to thee.
Some will wonder how I so willingly can say good-bye
to the Corporate monopoly.

Good - bye to stress and sleepless nights.
Good - bye to all the pressure and hype.
Good - bye to endless work
all too much for sanity's plight.
Good - bye. Good - bye. I kiss you Good - bye.

No more! No more!   Nevermore!

You own me no more.

Some will say,

 How could she leave such a good job?

What about retirement?

It's not a good time to quit your job,

The economy is not good.....

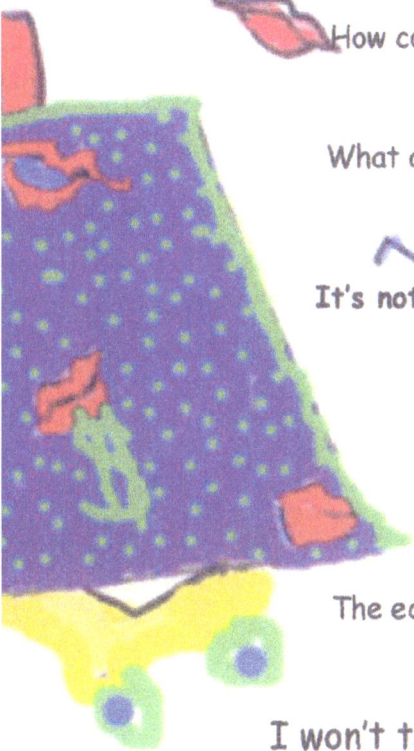

I won't try to explain and I'll finally

be able to sleep.

I'm out of words.

I'm out of wind.

I'm out...

having fun!

The
End

64

www.ingramcontent.com/pod-product-compliance
Lightning Source LLC
Chambersburg PA
CBHW041404090426
42744CB00001B/2